REVIEW OF

## With Dignity And Honor

BY ROBERTO ALMANZÁN
Diversity Trainer & Consultant
Cast member of *The Color of Fear*

Our nation is rapidly becoming a multiracial, multiethnic, and multicultural nation. All demographic projections visualize European Americans becoming a minority in this country, the only unknown is how soon this will occur. Several years ago in California, students of color exceeded 50 percent of the public school population; and, just recently, the population of people of color exceeded that of European Americans.

Many Americans are not prepared for the changes brought on by this demographic transformation and feel uncomfortable and sometimes even frightened, threatened, and angry. Eurocentrism and racism are the source of these feelings of uneasiness, anxiety and fear. Transcending a Eurocentric dream of America, unlearning racism, and becoming informed about and learning to value ethnic diversity—all human diversity—are the elements necessary for a successful evolution into a multicultural future. Successfully managing this multicultural evolution may be the greatest challenge our nation faces as it enters the Twenty-first century.

Preston Che Ping Ni, an instructor at Foothill College in Northern California, has written an excellent introductory text for students who are learning about ethnic diversity and the challenges involved in becoming a multicultural society. The book's format should appeal to students raised on MTV: with bold print, a lot of white space, short paragraphs, many potent quotations, and concise chapters. It is a fast read, moving along this terrain at a rapid clip.

In this short, well organized book, the author uses a chapter to cover all the definitions necessary to begin to understand racism and to discuss the issues. In a subsequent chapter, Preston Ni presents eight concepts that help readers understand important diversity issues. One premise is that this work, of unlearning racism and appreciating diversity, is not about blaming and bashing white people, but about uncovering and unlearning the attitudes and thought patterns that support racism. Another idea, extremely important in my experience, is that indifference is one of the major attitudes that hinders progress. Some of the ways I have heard this attitude expressed by non-target people is it doesn't happen to me, everybody has a hard life, or not wanting to offend friends or co-workers. Some of the other concepts covered are white privilege, understanding the history of Americans of color, the impact of the media on stereotypes and ideal images, and discrimination between ethnic groups.

Additional chapters are devoted to actions the individual can take to repudiate racism and, especially relevant for students, how education and a proactive stance can be empowering. Quotations on concepts relevant to racism make up one of the last chapters. An example is this powerful quotation from Elie Weisel, "Indifference . . . is the epitome of evil. The opposite of love is not hate, it's indifference . . . ." Another one comes from the National Spiritual Assembly of The Baha'is of the United States, ". . . the transformation of a whole nation ultimately depends on the initiative and change of character of the individuals who compose it." The last chapter presents sample teaching activities that students can engage in to further their understanding of ethnicity, culture, diversity, and racism.

This is what the work of eliminating racism and valuing diversity is about, step by step, person by person, educating and raising the awareness of all Americans. Sometimes this seems like such an overwhelming task, but as Preston Ni quotes Toni Cade Bambera, "The dream is real my friends. The failure to make it work is the unreality." This book can help college students, and other readers, take a step to make the dream real.

# WITH
# DIGNITY
*and*
# HONOR

*Understanding Racism*

*Unlearning Racism*

Second Edition

Preston Che Ping Ni, M.S.B.A

**Burgess Publishing**
*A Division of Burgess International Group, Inc.*

**Also by Preston Che Ping Ni**
HOW TO DEAL WITH CONFLICT AND HANDLE DIFFICULT PEOPLE

Content Layout Design: Shelley A. Schreiber

Printed in the United States of America.
J  I  H  G  F  E  D

Address orders to:

BURGESS INTERNATIONAL GROUP, Inc.
7110 Ohms Lane
Edina, Minnesota 55439-2143
Telephone 612-820-4561
Toll Free 1-800-356-6826
Fax 612/831-3167

Burgess Publishing
A Division of BURGESS INTERNATIONAL GROUP, Inc.

# Acknowledgments

*James Baldocchi, Robert Gardner, Rick Herbert, Stuart Krantz, Lisa Nakamura, Bonnie Zeltmann, Michille Akhavi, Scott Lankford, Rowena Matsunari, George McKinney, Jim Seyfert, M. Tran, Br. Phillip K., May Tung, Sarah Pearson, San Francisco Men's Tribe, and the students, faculty and staff of Foothill College*

*The Dream is Alive . . .*

"So long as there shall exist, by reason of law and custom, a social condemnation which, in the midst of civilization, artificially creates a hell on earth, and complicates with human fatality a destiny that is divine . . . so long as, in certain regions, social asphyxia shall be possible . . . so long as ignorance and misery remain on earth . . . ."

—*Haunteville House*

Our deepest fear is not that we
are inadequate.

Our deepest fear is that we are powerful
beyond measure.

It is our light, not our darkness, that most
frightens us.

We ask ourselves, who am I to be brilliant,
gorgeous, talented, and fabulous?

Actually, who are you NOT to be?

You are a child of the universe.

Your playing small doesn't serve the world.

There's nothing enlightened about shrinking
so that other people won't feel insecure
around you.

We were born to manifest the glory that is
within us.

It's not just in some of us; it's in everyone.

As we let our own light shine, we
unconsciously give other people permission
to do the same.

As we are liberated from our own fear, our
presence automatically liberates others.

—*quoted by Nelson Mandela*
*1994 Inaugural Speech*

"Tell me whom you love, and I will tell you who you are."

—*Houssaye*

# WITH
# DIGNITY
## *and*
# HONOR

## Table of Contents

# PART THREE: *Unlearning Racism*

# PART ONE:

*With Liberty And Justice For All*

# CHAPTER ONE:

*Our Inalienable Rights*

"We hold these truths to be self-evident, that all men are created equal, that they are endowed by their Creator with certain inalienable rights, that among these are Life, Liberty, and the pursuit of Happiness— that to secure these rights, Governments are instituted among Men, deriving their just powers from the consent of the governed . . ."

*—from "The United States Declaration of Independence"*

"Congress shall make no law respecting an establishment of religion, or prohibiting the free exercise thereof; or abridging the freedom of speech, or of the press, or the right of the people peaceably to assemble, and to petition the government for a redress of grievances."

*—from "The First Amendment of The United States Constitution"*

## Fundamental Human Rights

We have these rights as long as we do not harm others. If we harm other people, then we forfeit our right to have these rights.

1. We have the right to be treated with respect.

2. We have the right to express our feelings, opinions, and wants.

3. We have the right to be listened to and be taken seriously.

4. We have the right to set our own priorities.

5. We have the right to say "no" without feeling guilty.

6. We have the right to get what we pay for.

7. We have the right to have our opinions different than others.

8. We have the right to take care and protect ourselves from being threatened physically, mentally, or emotionally.

In the United States, our Constitution, our Bill of Rights, our democratic process, and our consumer protection laws assume these rights for all, regardless of our sex, culture, age, religion, or class. Although some people in our society do not respect these rights, in the United States we have the right to fight for these rights.

More importantly, we have these rights because we say so. If we believe we are worthy and deserving of respect, then we will live our lives and conduct ourselves accordingly. If we do not believe we are worthy of these rights, then we have lost no matter what measure of protection society brings us.

# PART TWO:
## Understanding Racism

# CHAPTER TWO:

## Concepts And Definitions

*The following concepts are defined from a multicultural relations and multicultural communication context*

## Culture

Distinct ways of life shared by a group of people and passed down from generation to generation; such as values, religion, language, holiday, lifestyle, communication style, cooking, etc. Although some cultural characteristics evolve from generation to generation, especially when one moves or immigrates to an area where another culture is the majority, many can stay the same over generations.

## Multiculturalism

The infusion of more than one cultural perspective in every single subject.

## Assimilation

Minority conforming to the majority culture in society for the sake of fitting in, often at the expense of losing part or all of one's cultural heritage.

## Ethnocentrism

Coming from one cultural perspective and excluding others; assuming one culture gets to establish the norms, therefore undermining other cultural perspectives. One can be ethnocentric regarding her/his own culture, or towards another culture (such as someone from outside the U.S. thinking: "everything about America is better; from its lifestyle to its pop culture," without critical examination). Ethnocentrism is often learned through the media and ethnocentrically-based school curriculum.

## *Stereotypes*

Generalization of race, gender, or sexual orientation that is untrue, often leads to prejudice, discrimination, and racism.

*Examples:* Media's frequent portrayal of African American men as violent and drug addicted, Asian women as quiet and subservient, Hispanic men as lazy and uneducated, Persian men as fanatical terrorists, blond women as lacking intelligence, and gay men as overly sensitive and feminine.

## Positive Stereotypes

Generalization of a cultural group which, although favorable sounding, actually undermines and harms members of the group because attention is diverted away from important issues.

*Example:* The stereotype that Asians are the "model minority" and "have made it" neglects the fact that hate crimes against people of Asian decent have increased dramatically in the 90's, that the average professional of Asian decent still receives less pay for the same position than her/his counterpart of European decent, and that large groups of Asians in the United States (such as many Southeast Asian refugees) are living at the poverty level and are in dire need of social assistance.

## *Prejudice*

An unfavorable notion toward certain
cultural/ethnic groups; a phenomenon often
learned from family, societal norms and
expectations, school curriculum, and the
media; maintaining a point of view which
contradicts facts; intolerance or hatred
toward other races.

"**BLACK:** Destitute of light, devoid of color, enveloped in darkness, hence utterly dismal or gloomy, as the future looked black, soiled with dirt, foul, sullen; hostile, forbidding, as a black day, outrageously wicked, as in black cruelty, indicating disgrace or dishonor."

"**WHITE:** Of the color of pure snow, reflecting all the rays of the spectrum, the opposite of black, free from a spot or a blemish, innocent, pure, without evil intent, harmless, honest, square dealing, honorable."

*—from the film "Malcolm X," quoting Webster's Collegiate Dictionary, Fifth edition.*

## Discrimination

The favoring of one group over another based on sex, culture, age, class, sexual orientation, or other factors in decision-making or in the distribution of power and/or resources.

*Examples of discrimination:* Many banks charge higher mortgage rates to seniors, women, minorities, and the poor; the *"glass ceiling"* phenomenon; income gap between genders and between people of different cultures, given the same position; more or less school funding based on demographics; real estate sales bias based on cultural exclusion in certain neighborhoods, etc.

## Racism

The use of racial prejudice and racial discrimination as a form of *power;* the dehumanization of a person based on race/culture; the abuse of political, social, legal, financial, informational, emotional and/or physical power to control, subjugate, exclude, or undermine people of specific cultural backgrounds.

*Examples of emotional abuse:* Insulting, belittling, ignoring, joking, labeling, yelling, resenting, blaming, accusing, name calling, social isolation, threatening retaliation, minimizing other's feelings, withholding emotional support.

### The difference between prejudice, discrimination, and racism:

Prejudice is an *attitude*.

Discrimination is *behavior* based on prejudice.

Racism is the use of racial prejudice and racial discrimination as *forms of power*.

## Conscious Racism

The practice of racism while being aware of one's own prejudice and/or discrimination.

## Unconscious racism

The practice of racism without awareness of one's own prejudice and/or discrimination.

*Examples:* Avoiding eye-contact with people of a specific cultural background without being aware of it, making fun of people from another culture without knowing that the remarks are prejudiced and hurtful, avoiding social interaction with members of a particular culture and claiming: "I've never even thought twice about it; it's just how it is, how things have always been."

*"I face racism (from) people who are good people, who are church-going, people who say they are my friends. These are the same people who make fun of my middle name, the way my parents talk, and pass me over in a restaurant in favor of a white person—not because they intentionally do so, but because I'm invisible to them."*

*—Edward Park*

## Overt Racism

The practice of racism that is clearly racially-based.

*Examples:* Using a racial slur, telling someone "go back to where you came from," racially motivated threat or violence; church burnings based on hate, etc.

## Covert Racism

The practice of racism that is subtle and unspoken. It is often difficult to discern for sure that racism is being practiced: the victim of this type of racism often feels uneasy, excluded, ignored, silenced, rejected, mistreated, uncomfortable, repressed, or undermined without necessarily knowing why. Many people who practice covert racism, consciously or unconsciously, will deny having any racist intentions when confronted on the matter.

*Examples:* Having an unspoken company policy of not hiring members of certain ethnicities, ignoring people of a particular culture for no justifiable reason while being friendly to everyone else, making services or memberships easier to obtain for some cultural groups than others; the "glass ceiling" phenomenon.

## Internalized Racism—Superior

An ingrained belief that one's *own* cultural group is more entitled, superior, beautiful, or "higher" in comparison to another cultural group, without critical examination; a phenomenon often learned from family upbringing, a dominant society/culture's norms and expectations, as well as media's positive or negative portrayal of certain cultural groups.

*"Where can I meet some Asian women? I want a woman who cooks for me, doesn't argue, and thinks I'm Tom Cruise!"*

*—Source Unknown,*
*Internet Chat Room*

### Internalized Racism—Inferior

An ingrained belief that one's own cultural group is undesirable, ugly, shameful, or "lower" in comparison to another cultural group, without critical examination. This is a phenomenon learned from family upbringing, a dominant society/culture's norms and expectations, as well as media's positive or negative portrayal of certain cultural groups.

Sometimes a person may have both types of internalized racism, such that she/he feels inferior when compared to one culture, and superior when compared to another.

## Examples of Inferior Internalized Racism

In Japan and China, as well as in parts of
Latin America, people undergo highly popular
cosmetic surgeries, such as "widening" of
their eyes, or removal of facial fat or even
bone fragments, in order to achieve a more
Caucasian look; finding one's own cultural
traditions, habits, and characteristics embar-
rassing or shameful in front of others. The
biased notion, usually learned from the
media and Hollywood, that men or women of
a dominant culture are more attractive and
desirable than men or women of one's own
culture; the tendency of some well-known
people of color in the fields of politics, sports,
and entertainment to abandon identifying
with, and reaching out to, their own ethnic
communities for the sake of fitting in with the
dominant culture/establishment; the notion
that everything "Western" or "American" is
better, without critical examination.

"All my life I thought white was more desirable—I even married a white man to feel better about myself. Today, many years later, I finally realized what I had done—in choosing skin color over character, I gave up the most precious parts of who I am: my cultural identity, my dignity, and my soul."

*—Asian American Woman*

## Institutional Racism

Overt or covert acts of racism practiced by an institution, such as government, police, church, educational institution, or business toward people of particular cultural backgrounds.

*"It is clear that American employers are more reluctant to hire blacks than any other group."*

—*Harry Holzer*

## Glass Ceiling

A phenomenon which describes the ability of underrepresented groups (minorities, women, gays, disabled, etc.) to achieve a middle level of career success, but not move higher due to individual and/or institutional racism. This is often apparent in business and government, where the great majority of executive and other positions of real power tend to be held by a particular ethnic and gender group.

*"My dad . . . came to a point where he couldn't get to where he wanted to get to (in the corporate world), and he wasn't sure it was because he was Chinese, but he wasn't sure it wasn't . . . . He's been told he was doing a great job, so what's going on? . . . by the time I was a teenager . . . he looked kind of beaten . . . like he lost."*

*—from "Stolen Ground"*

## Diversity

The recognition of cultural plurality in our society; the embodiment of cultural communities geographically, socially, and culturally.

## Segregation

Geographical, social, and cultural separation between cultural groups, who nevertheless dwell over a common landscape.

# CHAPTER THREE:

*Eight Ideas Concerning Cultural
Relations and Racism In The United
States Today*

## *Idea #1 — Not Against Whites*

Taking a stand against racism is not about
taking a stand against people of European
descent (white people). Fighting racism is
fighting an attitude and an institutionalized
condition which consciously and unconsciously assume that one group is superior,
more privileged, more desirable, or "higher"
than others simply because of their ethnicity.
It is this attitude and this condition against
which we must take a stand.

## Idea #2 — U.S. History: Past and Present

The United States of America has a very racist history. We were one of the last countries in the world to abolish slavery. Less than 40 years ago, The United States and South Africa were the only two countries in the world where a person of African descent could not, by law, eat, drink, sit, or wash their hands at places designated "whites only." San Francisco, with one of the largest Asian communities in the United States, confined its Chinese and Chinese American residents to eight square blocks of Chinatown until the end of World War II.

Today, the United States is still strongly influenced by this history. Some Native Americans still live on reservations. African Americans are still treated as second-class citizens. Second-, third-, fourth-generation Americans of non-European descent are still looked upon and treated as foreigners in their own country. The "glass ceiling" phenomenon toward minorities, women, and other underrepresented groups is still pervasive throughout government and business.

When World War II was declared

on the morning radio,

we glued our ears, widened our eyes.

Our bodies shivered . . .

Shortly our Japanese neighbors vanished,

and my parents continued to whisper:

We are Chinese, we are Chinese

We wore black arm bands,

put up a sign

in bold letters.

—*Author Unknown*

The World War II internment of Japanese
Americans (JAs) partly explains why . . .


Many JAs are not interested in their
Japanese heritage

The out marriage rate for JA women is the
highest of any minority group (50-70%)

JAs appear so assimilated

The house I grew up in looked like white
Americans lived there

I once chewed my younger brother out for eat-
ing Japanese rice crackers in front of my
white friends from school

I was rude to my JA elementary teachers

My mother to this day wipes her silverware off
in restaurants before using it

I went to Japan to find part of myself

I became an educator

—*Lori Kuwabara*

And yes I cried . . . I had a house to live in, even though many times I felt not wanted there. I saw our men gather on the corners very early in the mornings, and I saw them leave by noon, for most of them have not gotten a job. I saw our women working very hard in housekeeping jobs. I saw my high school friends drop out of school because they could no longer keep up with a full-time job and the school demands. I saw our children: confused, shy, and quiet. And I heard the news: children being born with birth defects due to the fertilizers used in the fields, where people worked for long hours for such low pay.

They all came searching for a better way of life. They all heard the story.

*—Foothill Student,*
*Mexican Descent*

"Is it so important . . . ? Let's look to the future!"

"It might scare you! Look at the past and learn for the future."

"Racism is the most challenging issue confronting America. To ignore the problem is to expose the country to physical, moral, and spiritual danger."

"America's peace, prosperity, and even her standing in the international community depend on healing the wounds of racism and building a society in which people of diverse backgrounds live as members of one family."

*—The National Spiritual Assembly of The Baha'is of the United States*

## Idea #3 — Indifference, the Opposite of Love

By not challenging the status quo, our indifference gives permission to continue the inequalities in our society. By enjoying our privileges without fighting for the rights of those who don't have them, we allow the injustice to continue. By not acknowledging and validating the experiences of those who have suffered, we elicit in others feelings of resentment and anger.

"The greatest force which perpetuates injustice is not hate. It is indifference."

—*Preston Che Ping Ni*


"When we hear a truth and do not act upon it, it becomes poison within ourselves."

—*J. Krishnamurti*

## Idea #4 — Using Blame and Fear

Blame and fear are two of the most effective ways of inciting racism. By blaming *an entire group of people* for the troubles of our society, leaders in politics, business, and the community get to avoid the difficult task of critically examining the real roots of our problems. By spreading fear that a certain group of people are threatening our society economically, socially, morally, or culturally, some people get to advance their own political expediencies.

*Examples:* Japanese American internment during W.W.II, overt anti-Semitism in the 50's, resistance to African American voting rights and desegregation in the 60's, Japan bashing in the 70's and 80's, immigrant bashing in the 90's.

## Idea #5 — Hollywood and the Media

Racism is also spread through the perpetuation of cultural stereotypes by Hollywood and the media. The media and Hollywood's portrayal of Caucasian women and men and their image and roles in relation to non-Caucasian women and men have caused profound influence on how we see ourselves and one another. From a very early age we are fed images of who has power, who's beautiful, and what is considered "human." Internalized racism, superior or inferior, is quickly formed.

"[As a Child, I] watched a lot of TV and movies, always with this subliminal discomfort that the only people I could identify with, I didn't identify with. So I was forced to identify with white role models."

—*B. D. Wong*

## Representation of African Americans

Dozens of studies have been done on the effects of television-watching on African American children. In after-school programs, only three percent of those who are involved in the production and acting of such programs are African American. African American children sorely lack positive role models on television, which in turn, as many of these studies show, affect their sense of positive self-identity, and, according to some, induces a feeling of genetic inferiority. In prime-time television, *lead* African American characters depicted as positive, intelligent, and non-comical are nearly non-existent. In Hollywood movies, African American males in their prime are most frequently portrayed as what Spike Lee's film, *Get on the Bus,* calls "the four R's: rap, rob, rape, and riot."

## Representation of Latinos and Latinas

Since the earliest Hollywood films, Latino men have been portrayed as law-breaking, lazy, dirty, immoral, uneducated, and untrustworthy (many "spaghetti westerns," many Cheech and Chong movies, *Clear and Present Danger, Con Air,* and many big budget Hollywood films' depiction of young, male Latino characters). The mascot on one popular brand of tortilla chips is "Banditos"— a Mexican bandit. One deodorant company produced a billboard advertisement featuring a scrubby-looking Mexican man. The caption: "If it works for him, it works for you." Middle-aged Latino women in Hollywood films are almost exclusively portrayed as maids or baby-sitters who speak broken English.

## Representation of Asian Men and Women

Asian women portrayed by Hollywood, television, and Broadway are often passive figures without character depth. Young Asian female characters are frequently scripted as love interests of Caucasian men *(Seven Years in Tibet, Mr. Baseball, Madam Butterfly, Miss Saigon, After M\*A\*S\*H,* even the so called "break through" productions such as *The Joy Luck Club,* and the short-lived television series, *All American Girl)*. The few U.S. commercials which feature both Asian and Caucasian men in their prime usually depict these men as competing for the affection of attractive Asian women (Budweiser beer, Command), with the Caucasian man the inevitable winner. Hollywood feature films routinely cast Asian men to look foolish, weak, and ridiculous in front of Caucasian men, especially when both are in the presence of attractive women *(Absolute Power, Beverly Hills Ninja, Breakfast at Tiffany's)*.

## Social Consequences of Media on Society

The effect of this type of media colonialism is that, after repeated exposure, both minority and Caucasian men and women begin to internalize these stereotypes and accept them as real. The boundary between media representation and reality becomes blurred, as people become, consciously or unconsciously, either the victims or the benefactors of such portrayals.

The result is often disheartening, saddening, and sometimes tragic:

One study shows that more African American children prefer to play with white dolls than with black dolls. Some African American women and, to a lesser degree now, men, spend large sums of money on hair procedures in order to have what appears to be naturally straight hair. Men and women of Latino descent are often discriminated against when interviewing for white collar positions because of the stereotype which automatically casts them as less educated and lazy. Some Latinos undergo surgery to remove fat pads from their eyes and cheeks to look "less ethnic," even though the surgery is considered risky. In survey after survey, Japanese women find white male celebrities more desirable than Asian male celebrities. "Wide eye" surgery is the most popular cosmetic surgery performed in Japan.

"Communication is always linked with power, that those groups who wield power in a society influence what gets represented through the media."

*—from Stuart Hall: "Representation and the Media"*

# Idea #6 — Class, Gender, and Other Variables

Prejudice, discrimination, and racism are complicated by economic class, gender, skin tone, sexuality and other variables, which individualize a person's experience of racism and discrimination.

*Example of economic class as a variable in racism/discrimination:* The lower the economic class, the more likely a person will experience overt racism (such as racial slurs, physical threats, etc.) The higher the economic class, the more likely a person will experience covert racism (such as glass ceiling, membership exclusion, etc.)

*Examples of gender as a variable in racism/ discrimination:* Racist attitude toward Asian and Latino men is often different than racist attitude toward Asian women and Latinas. Racist attitude toward Asian and Latino men is often expressed to *suppress* and *demasculinize* their male identity (characterizing Asian men as nerdy, weak (yellow), and lacking charisma; characterizing Latino men as lazy, uneducated, and unfaithful). On the other hand, racist attitude toward Asian women and Latinas is often expressed to *exploit* and *objectify* their stereotyped femininity (Asian women as doll-like, quiet, submissive, and compliant; Latinas as sexy, passionate, lustful, and "hot" objects of desire).

In both cases, these racist attitudes serve to have power over the men, and disempower the women.


"She's like a delicate China doll . . . she's like one of those porcelain figurines that mom collects. She's so pure and delicate and innocent . . . you just have to look at her, and you want to take care of her the rest of your life."

*—from "To Die For"*

# Idea #7 — The Invisible Privilege

Privilege can be defined as social, economical, psychological, or political rights, benefits, comforts, and/or acceptance granted to a person or a group, but denied to others.

Living in the United States, many (not all) Caucasians have a different experience than many "people of color." Much of this difference in experience comes from being able to take certain rights, benefits, comforts, and/or social acceptance for granted that a person of color cannot. This "invisible" privilege, which many Euro-Americans are unaware of, is also varied by gender and economic class.

*"Race. It's not something whites think about, except occasionally . . . . Blacks do not have that luxury. They are made aware of race day in and day out. And it is that privilege of not having to be aware, that 'whiteness of whiteness,' that . . . we must get past if we are to ever end racism in this country."*

—Rebecca Parr

A sample questionnaire to see whether you might have certain privileges others may not:

1. I can turn on the television and easily find *lead* characters of my skin color and "race" portrayed in a positive and non-comical manner.

2. I can travel to most places in the United States without worrying about physical threat or blatant discrimination.

3. I can find in U.S. history books numerous mentions of the positive contributions made by people of my "race."

4. I can be successful in what I do and not be labeled as "a credit to my race." (which, intentionally or unintentionally, implies "you're better than the rest of your race")

5. I don't have to deal with people saying "go back to where you came from!"

6. I can eat like a slob in a restaurant and not have my behavior attributed to my ethnicity.

7. I can easily find flesh-color bandages that pretty much match my skin tone.

8. I can read advertisements for holiday resorts and boat cruises and easily find people of my "race" pictured as welcomed guests.

9. I don't have to deal with others stereotyping and laughing at how people from my cultural group speak English.

10. I can easily find representations of God and angels that look similar to my "race."

"... white people expect more out of people of color, service wise, than they would of other whites. Many (of my classmates of color tell me that) these acts are degrading to them, even though they understand that most white people don't realize when they are doing it."

—*Jeremy Van Wert*


"(As a white person) if I work hard . . . I'm going to get what I want. For some other cultures in our society that's not true . . . they have to work twice as hard . . . and there's people (who) tell them they can't."

—*from "Skin Deep"*


"When I stand in line (at) the counter to be served . . . and the white person who comes after me gets served first, it's not done on purpose. It's because the person doesn't see me . . . . I'm invisible to that white person."

—*from "The Color of Fear"*

## Idea #8 — Discrimination Among Minority Groups

There is prejudice and discrimination among minority groups in the United States. Many minorities think little of the plight of African Americans. African Americans often perceive Asians as siding with Caucasians. There is tension between Latinos and African Americans. There is misplaced anger and blame between minority groups (Example: The hostilities between African Americans and Korean grocers during the Los Angeles "riots"). Also, many newly arrived immigrants have already had exposure to prejudices and stereotypes in their own countries (through media, Hollywood, etc.), and are quick to further internalize superior or inferior racism once they are in the U.S.

"Although my parents felt inferior because they were so disrespected by the whites, they always consoled themselves by saying that at least they were better than the blacks."

"We compare ourselves in relation to whites. We put each other down for not being white."

—*Anonymous*

# PART THREE:

*Unlearning Racism*

# CHAPTER FOUR:

*Large and Small Acts to Help Dissolve
Cultural Barriers*

## See People As Individuals

See people who are different than you as individuals, not as a group. Base your relationship with them on individual character, not group stereotypes.

*"If I go out and I shop lift, the first thing that happens when . . . whomever sees me (is to think): 'Well, you know they all shop lift!' And every black person in that store at that point in time (will think): 'Damn!' "*

*". . . because it has an effect on 22 million African Americans in this country. If one black person does something, we all suffer— every last one of us."*

*—from "Skin Deep"*

## Teach Your Children Well

If it applies, be the first generation in your family to put a stop to racism. Teach your children the values of justice and equality.

*"Racism is a family tradition. The family is where one learns one's values and morals; if the family teaches its Children to hate, then they will continue the tradition. We focus too much on the adult dilemma of racism and not enough on the child who is potentially a racist."*

*"The only solution to ending racism is to give children another outlet . . . to learn that racism is wrong. If we can accomplish this, than we can break the chain of hatred in the family."*

—Michille Akhavi

## *It All Begins With a Smile . . .*

"Fear of people stems from the lack of knowledge and lack of previous personal contact. If I just stand by and watch or avoid being close to a particular type of person, these persons I put into a certain category will never become my friends. I may not be able to find anything clever to say, but saying only 'Hi!' could be a good place to start."

—*Kazuko Enda*

## A Smile

It costs nothing but creates much.

It enriches those who receive, without impoverishing those who give.

It happens in a flash and the memory of it sometimes lasts forever.

None are so rich that they can get along without it, and none are so poor but are richer for a smile.

Yet it cannot be bought, begged, borrowed or stolen, for it is something that is no earthly good to anyone until it is given away.

*—Source Unknown*

## Small Groups, Common Goals

There's nothing like a common goal which brings people of diverse backgrounds together. Seek out opportunities to work with people from different backgrounds in school, at work, and in the community. Such groups help expand perspectives and friendships.

*"No real change will come about without close association, fellowship, and friendship among diverse peoples."*

*—The National Spiritual Assembly of The Baha'is of the United States*

## "Don't Do It !"

Most of us have probably told racist jokes to our friends and have been told many more. It's easy to tell a racist joke and get a quick laugh, and easier still to listen to one and laugh along.

Every time we make a joke at another culture's expense, or listen to one without protest, we give social permission to ourselves and others to continue discrimination over and over again.

This social permission will exist unless you stop it, and tell your friends to stop it:

"Don't do it!"

"Do you really mean that?"

"Then why did you say that?"

"This is not cool with me!"


*"I just want you to stop doing this. I want you to stop hurting me."*

*—Lee Mun Wah*

## Validate Feelings

To validate feelings is to recognize the emotions of a person, and to acknowledge that these feelings are really happening to that person.

We can validate feelings even if we don't agree with the person, or understand the basis for her/his feelings:

"I know you're angry about this . . ."

"I can see that you're really upset . . ."

Validation of a person's feelings is an important element in the resolution of grievances. As you acknowledge a person's feelings, you help dissolve her/his emotional intensity around the subject, thus creating an opening to discuss the issue at hand.

*"We do need to get that anger out . . .*
*underneath all that anger is all that hurt that*
*has never been allowed to come out for us.*
*And on the other end . . . is a possibility."*

*—Lee Mun Wah*

## *Knowledge is Power*

Know your family history.

Understand United States history as the story of many cultures.

Recognize the contributions of each cultural group, as well as the injustices committed toward other cultural groups.

Develop awareness of the many inequalities and injustices which still exist in our society today.

Scrutinize media and Hollywood representation of people of different cultures.

Discern the difference between stereotype and reality.

"Finding the occasional straw of truth awash in a great ocean of confusion and bamboozle requires intelligence, vigilance, dedication and courage. But if we don't practice these tough habits of thought, we cannot hope to solve the truly serious problems that face us—and we risk becoming a nation of suckers, up for grabs by the next charlatan who comes along."

—*Carl Sagan,*
*"The Fine Art of Baloney Detection"*

## Actions A to Z

| | |
|---|---|
| **Act** | boldly |
| **Be** | an example of integrity |
| **Care** | about those less fortunate than you |
| **Dare** | to interrupt acts of injustice |
| **Engage** | in group activities with common goals |
| **Find** | the good in everyone |
| **Generate** | the spirit of kindness and acceptance |
| **Have** | a sense of humor about our crazy world |
| **Include** | friendships from everywhere and every culture |
| **Join** | a volunteer group |
| **Know** | the contributions of America's diverse people |
| **Love** | your enemy, for love makes you strong |

| | |
|---|---|
| **Make** | an effort to reach out |
| **Never** | succumb to hate |
| **Parent** | your children well |
| **Question** | stereotypes |
| **Run** | for leadership positions: healthy power empowers |
| **Speak** | from your heart |
| **Teach** | to broaden minds |
| **Urge** | people to vote |
| **Vote** | for those who show fairness and compassion |
| **Walk** | your talk |
| **Xenophilia** | (a love of people and things strange and foreign)—not xenophobia (fear of the same) |
| **Yield** | your ethnocentricity |
| **Zero** | tolerance for hate |

# CHAPTER FIVE:

*Pathways Toward Personal and*
*Social Empowerment*

## Empowerment
## through Education

- Finish high school

- Get a college education

- Develop strong oral communication skills

- Develop strong written communication skills

- Take courses in ethnic studies, women's studies, and other perspective-expanding subjects

- Get involved in campus organizations

- Participate in student government

- Acquire an internship

When you reach your goals, give something back to help empower the next generation.

"Education in the principle of the oneness of humanity is the shortest route out of poverty and prejudice."

—*The National Spiritual Assembly of The Baha'is of the United States*

"Education is dangerous . . . . Every educated person is a future enemy . . . . We are the master."

—*Official Nazi Policy on the Enslavement of Subjugated People, 1942*

## *Empowerment through Local Action*

- Vote

- Register people to vote

- Volunteer

- Be active in your local community

- Write your Congressman/Congresswoman

- Write editorials to newspapers
  and magazines

- Speak out on television and radio's public
  service announcements

- Be a big brother/big sister—role models
  change lives

- Contribute to worthy causes

- Accept, or run for leadership roles (as
  committee member, board of director, etc.)

- Join a local *Toastmasters* to improve your
  communication skills

- Attend and/or participate in cultural
  events, festivals, and discussions

This is the true joy in life, the being used for a purpose recognized by yourself as a mighty one; the being force of nature instead of a feverish, selfish little clod of ailments and grievances complaining that the world will not devote itself to making you happy.

I am of the opinion that my life belongs to the whole community, and as long as I live, it is my privilege to do for it whatever I can.

I want to be thoroughly used up when I die, for the harder I work, the more I live. I rejoice in life for its own sake. Life is no "brief candle" to me. It is a sort of bright torch which I have got hold of for the moment and I want to make it burn as brightly as possible before handing it on to future generations.

—*G. Bernard Shaw*

# CHAPTER SIX:

## *Mindful Quotes*

## On Oneness

"The fundamental solution to racial and ethnic conflict rests ultimately on the common recognition of the oneness of humankind . . . . The oneness of humanity, a spiritual truth abundantly confirmed by science, implies an organic change in the structure of present-day society."

*—The National Spiritual Assembly of The Baha'is of the United States*

"Calculations of the slow changes that take place in human DNA over the millennia indicate that everyone alive today may be a descendant of a single female ancestor who lived in Africa 140,000 to 280,000 years ago, scientists at the University of California have reported."

*— Working Women*
*September, 1986*

"I can see myself in all things and all people around me."

*—Sanskrit Phrase*

## *On Love*

"Love is mightier than hate."

*—Preston Che Ping Ni*

"Love is or it ain't."

*—Toni Morrison*

"You have a different kind of tenderness for everybody you know."

*—Allan Gurganus*

"We can truly love someone only to the extent that we accept ourselves."

"We can purposely hurt someone only to the extent that we have not come to terms with our own pain."

—Preston Che Ping Ni

"I love you more than my own skin."

—Frida Kahlo

"In focusing on others' needs, we also discover meaning beyond the self. The New Testament's four books on Jesus' life all record his teaching that to find life we must be willing to lose our lives. To find meaning we must discover something bigger than ourselves, and serve it."

*— David G. Myers*


"Nothing makes you happier than when you really reach out in mercy to someone who is badly hurt."

*—Mother Teresa*

## On Diversity

"The history of the United States is the story of people of many backgrounds."

—*William Loren Katz*

"A lot of different flowers make a bouquet."

—*Muslim Origin*

"Complaining about too much diversity is like complaining about too many colors in the rainbow."

—*Preston Che Ping Ni*

Archie Bunker: *"What color was he?"*

His young niece: *"People color."*

—*from "All in the Family"*

## On Justice

"But the meek shall inherit the earth; and shall delight themselves in the abundance of peace."

—*Psalm 37:11*


"When I despair, I remember that all through history, the way of truth and love has always won. There have been tyrants and murderers and for a time they can seem invincible, but in the end they always fall."

—*Mahatma Gandhi*

"There is no black problem. The real problem is whether or not the American people have the honor enough, the courage enough, the loyalty enough, to simply live up to their own constitution."

—*Frederick Douglass*

"As I would not be a slave, so I would not be a master. This expresses my idea of democracy. Whatever differs from this, to the extent of the difference, is not democracy."

—*Abraham Lincoln*

## On Injustice

"To be a Negro in this country and to be
relatively conscious is to be in rage most of
the time."

—*James Baldwin*


"That man over there says women need to be
helped into carriages and lifted over ditches,
and to have the best place everywhere.
Nobody ever helps me into carriages or over
puddles, or gives me the best place, and ain't I
a woman? Look at my arm! I have ploughed
and planted and gathered into barns and no
man could head me, and ain't I a woman? I
could work as much and eat as much as a man
when I could get it and bear the lash as well!
And ain't I a woman? I have borne thirteen
children and seen most of 'em sold into
slavery and when I cried out with my
mother's grief none but Jesus heard me
and ain't I a woman?"

—*Sojourner Truth*

## On Indifference

"The only thing necessary for the triumph of evil is for good men to do nothing."

—*Edmund Burke*


"Indifference, to me, is the epitome of evil. The opposite of love is not hate, it's indifference. The opposite of faith is not heresy, it's indifference. And the opposite of life is not death, it's indifference. Because of indifference, one dies before one actually dies. To be in the window and watch people being sent to concentration camps or being attacked in the street and do nothing, that's being dead."

—*Elie Weisel*

"What luck for rulers that men do not think."

—*Adolf Hitler*


"In Germany they came first for the Communists, and I didn't speak up because I wasn't a Communist. Then, they came for the Jews and I didn't speak up because I wasn't a Jew. Then they came for the trade unionist, and I didn't speak up because I wasn't a trade unionist. Then they came for the Catholics and I didn't speak up because I was a Protestant. Then they came for me, and by that time no one was left to speak up."

—*Pastor Martin Niemoller*
*Nazi Victim*

## On Taking Action

"Where there's injustice, I always believe in fighting. The question is: do you fight to change things, or do you fight to punish? For myself I've found with all such sin as we should leave punishment to God."

—*Mahatma Gandhi*

"I thought, for years, that the proper response to evil policies was a polite response. Don't make waves. Even when I was boiling inside, I was smiling—trying stupidly to ignore oppressive institutional failure, believing if I was nice enough, maybe it would correct itself . . . . I should have fought back—placidly, yes, but actively."

—*Patricia Raybon*

"If there is no struggle, there is no progress. Those who profess to favor freedom and yet depreciate agitation are men who want crops without plowing up the ground, they want rain without thunder and lightening . . . . Find out just what any people will quietly submit to and you have found out the exact measure of injustice and wrong which will be imposed upon them, and these will continue until they are resisted with either words or blows, or with both."

—*Frederick Douglass*

"Progress in humanity, I believe, is made by those who face seemingly insurmountable odds and make a difference which changes the course of humankind."

—*Preston Che Ping Ni*

## On Tolerance

"The test of courage comes when we are in the minority; the test of tolerance comes when we are in the majority."

—*Ralph W. Sockman*

"Where each man claims his freedom as a matter of right, the freedom he accords to other men is a matter of toleration."

—*Walter Lippmann*

"You can't hold a man down without staying down with him."

—*Booker T. Washington*

## On Attitude

"If you don't have the capacity to change yourself and your own attitudes, then nothing around you can be changed."

*—Anwar Sadat, quoting the Koran*

"What you think, you become."

*—Mahatma Gandhi*

"If we don't accept ourselves for who we are
and where we've come from, who will?"

—*Silvia Rojas*

"To be yourself, you must first get
over yourself."

—*Preston Che Ping Ni*

## I Believe

I believe that love is mightier than hate;
Courage triumphs over fear.

I believe that we are limited by the scope of
our imagination;
Our lives go as far as our vision.

I believe that love is to give;
Through giving we reveal the breadth of our
character and the depth of our soul.

I believe in magic;
Creating new possibilities in the midst of
seeming impossibilities.

Finally, I believe that you and I are ONE;
Differences, boundaries, and separations are
merely myths over our common bond.

—*Preston Che Ping Ni*

### On Having Fun

"A recent Ku Klux Klan rally in Austin produced an eccentric counter-demonstration. When the fifty Klansmen appeared in front of the state capitol, they were greeted by five thousand locals who had turned out for a "Moon the Klan" rally. Citizens dropped by both singly and in groups, occasionally producing a splendid wave effect. It was a swell do."

"You got to have fun while you're fightin' for freedom, 'cause you don't always win . . . And when you get through kickin' ass and celebratin' the sheer joy of a good fight, be sure to tell those who come after how much fun it was."

—*Molly Ivins*

"Nothing dissolves tension and gives permission to dialogue like good-natured humor. We're much more likely to make progress if we can laugh together along the way."

—*Preston Che Ping Ni*

### Unclear on the Concept Winners:

"I'm American—I have no cultural background."

"Music 101 discussion topic: which piano keys are superior; ebony or ivory?"

"We're not studying ethnic literature; we're studying *Irish* literature."

"I believe we should definitely get more diversity into our organization: we need more Mexicans; we need more blacks; and we could use (looking at the author) one more Chinese!"

## On Freedom and Liberation

"Those who deny freedom to others deserve it not for themselves."

*—Source Unknown*

"You can kill a man, but you can't kill an idea."

*—Medgar Evers*

"Beyond the walls, the fears, the unspoken and subtle bias, is personal liberation."

*—Preston Che Ping Ni*

## On Hope and Optimism

"I am fundamentally an optimist . . . . Part of being optimistic is keeping one's head pointed toward the sun, one's feet moving forward. There were many dark moments when my faith in humanity was sorely tested, but I would not and could not give myself up to despair. That way lay defeat and death."

—*Nelson Mandela*


"The harshest winter finds an invincible summer in us."

—*Albert Camus*

## On Courage and Perseverance

"Character cannot be developed in ease and quiet. Only through experience of trial and suffering can the soul be strengthened, vision cleared, ambition inspired and success achieved."

—*Helen Keller*

"I am not discouraged, because every wrong attempt discarded is another step forward."

—*Thomas Edison*

"Abraham Lincoln lost eight elections, failed twice in business and suffered a nervous breakdown before he became the president of the United States."

—*Wall Street Journal, by United Technologies Corp.*

"The marvelous richness of human experience would lose something of rewarding joy if there were no limitations to overcome. The hilltop hour would not be half so wonderful if there were no dark valleys to traverse."

—*Helen Keller*

## *On Personal Responsibility*

"We appeal to the individual American because the transformation of a whole nation ultimately depends on the initiative and change of character of the individuals who compose it."

—*The National Spiritual Assembly of the Baha'is of the United States*

"Liberty means responsibility. That is why most men dread it."

—*George Bernard Shaw*

"The dream is real my friends. The failure to make it work is the unreality."

—*Toni Cade Bambera*

"I grew up in a family that could not see past the color line. To me, one of the most important accomplishments in my life is to know that I have broken the chain of racism in my family."

—*Michille Akhavi*


"We ourselves feel that what we are doing is just a drop in the ocean. But the ocean would be less because of that missing drop."

—*Mother Teresa*

## On Spiritual Medicine

"If we take the world's enduring religions at their best, we discover the distilled wisdom of the human race."

—*Huston Smith*

"When they say come and sing, that's the medicine."

—*Ella Fitzgerald*

"When you've got too much religion that you can't mingle with people, that you're afraid of certain people, you've got too much religion."

—*C. L. Franklin*

## On Self-Knowledge

"You shall know the truth, and the truth shall make you free."

—*John, Ch. 8*

"The true value of a human being can be found to the degree to which he has attained liberation from the self."

— *Albert Einstein*

"Look within yourself. After self-reflection, one's eyes may open and see things in an honest light, and view people and things with appreciation for all their natural beauty."

—*Tao Principle*

"But first I have to go to the place, move the dirt, find why I am here."

—*Toni Morrison*

"The man who sweats under his mask, whose role makes him itch with discomfort, who hates the division in himself, is already beginning to be free."

—*Thomas Merton*

"... education about the causes of oppression and the understanding of people's differences is critical in finding a peaceful solution . . . ."

*—Author Unknown*

"Those who do not remember the past are condemned to relive it."

*— Santayana*

"Where do we come from?

Who are we?

Where are we going?"

—Gauguin

## On Forgiveness

"Please forgive us. Please release and please set into the depth of the ocean our pilikia (trouble), nevermore to rise. All this we ask in Thy holy name. Amen."

*—E. Victoria Shook,
Ho'oponopono: Contemporary
Uses of a Hawaiian
Problem-Solving Process*

"You can only forgive others for their trespasses to the extent that you have forgiven yourself for allowing them to trespass against you."

*—Preston Che Ping Ni*

"Because in spite of everything, I still believe that people are really good at heart."

—*Anne Frank*

# Chapter Seven:

*Sample Teaching Activities*
*and Exercises*

*(The following are some of the assignments*
*used in the author's Intercultural Communication*
*class at Foothill College)*

# CULTURAL EXPERIENCE

**Purpose:** To engage in open and authentic sharing of cultural experiences.

**Length:** 5 minutes per student

Share with the class a cultural experience which has had a significant effect in your life. It can be an experience with someone who's different than you, or a time when you immersed yourself in a different cultural environment. Your experience can be positive, challenging, negative, or a mixture of all. Don't talk about something rather superficial and light; really think about your experiences and pick one that moves/stirs you, so that your communication will be a valuable experience for both you and the class. Examples: personal cultural experience involving friendship, relationship, travel, immigration, racism/discrimination, language difficulty, unique cultural experiences such as religious service, holiday, etc.

Tell us what you learned from this cultural experience, and whether it influenced how you see and relate to people/cultures that are different than you. If you can, bring with you an object which for you represents that experience (such as photograph, passport, jewelry, green card, dictionary, gift, etc.). Pass the object around in class as you share your personal intercultural story.

Each time we express ourselves openly and authentically, we create an opportunity to learn more about ourselves, and for others to understand more of who we are. Let this presentation be your first attempt at creating meaningful and in-depth "true dialogue" with your classmates. To a large degree this exercise will set the tone for everything else we do in the class.

**Tips on successfully completing this assignment:**

1. Be yourself—share with the class your thoughts and feelings. Express yourself!

2. Speak from your gut—talk about something that was very important to you or had a strong impact on you, even if you're not completely comfortable talking about it. You'll know you've found a good experience to share if the experience hits you at a "gut" level.

3. Speak from your heart—sincerely express something true and dear to you.

4. Personal story—share your experience in the form of a personal story.

5. Humor—if it feels natural, don't be afraid to be funny.

# CULTURAL JOURNAL

**Number of Entries:** Minimum 1 per week, beginning the first week of quarter, up to 3 entries per week. Date each entry.

**Length:** Minimum one page (on letter size paper) per entry; either single-spaced, hand-written or double-spaced typed either 10-, 11- or 12-point font.

**Possible Journal Topics:**

- Your experience of yourself and others in the class.
- Your intercultural communication-related experiences outside of class.
- Relating what we discuss/learn in class to your outside experience.
- Your thoughts, feelings, questions, issues and explorations concerning your own cultural identity, in general, and your cultural identity in the United States, in particular.
- Your experience participating in discussions, presentations, group work, and other activities in class.
- Your thoughts and feelings relating to the readings and assignments.
- Your thoughts and feelings regarding the videos screened in class.
- What you are learning about yourself, others, and from the class, in general.

In general, your entry topics will be satisfactory as long as they relate to your intercultural experiences in or outside of class.

**Confidentiality:** Only I will read your journal entries, and I will not discuss or show any part of your journal to anyone else unless I ask you specifically for permission. Be honest, thoughtful, and in-depth with what you write. Don't try to say the "right" thing, or what you think I like to hear. Effective communication begins with how you communicate with yourself, and your honesty with your thoughts and feelings is the first step.

**Quality of Writing:** While you do not have to produce perfectly written essays for each entry, I do expect that you express your thoughts clearly, that your English is basically correct, and your writing (if by hand) legible. If I can not follow your ideas, or see too many language mistakes, or cannot read your writing, you will receive partial or no credit for such entries.

**Grading:** Grading will be based on the consistency (at least 1 every week, not all in the last few weeks of the quarter), honesty, thoughtfulness, insightfulness, depth, and written quality of your entries.

If you have any questions concerning this assignment, please see me.

> *"Take this as a diary. Or a journal. Or a journey:*
>
> *A long ride back, with stops along the way to sort things out—then forgive them, then forget them. Then it's time to move on."*
>
> *—Patricia Raybon*

> *"It is the moment of truth. I cannot lie to me."*
>
> *—Duke Ellington*

# WRITING ASSIGNMENT: MULTICULTURAL CONCEPTS

**Procedure:**

1. Rent the movie *Lone Star*, hailed by some as *"America's soul-search for its national and cultural identity."*

2. Relate the movie to the concepts listed below (refer to Chapter Two for definitions). For each concept, write down at least one example from the movie which illustrates the idea. Be sure you briefly describe the scene and then explain how the scene is an example of a particular concept. The more thoughtful and in-depth your explanation is, the better.

1. Multiculturalism
2. Assimilation
3. Ethnocentrism
4. Prejudice
5. Discrimination
6. Racism
7. Emotional Abuse
8. Unconscious Racism
9. Internalized Racism: Superior
10. Internalized Racism: Inferior
11. Institutional Racism
12. Glass Ceiling
13. Diversity
14. Segregation

**For example: 11.** In the movie, Sheriff Ward's police department practiced overt <u>institutional racism</u> through physical and emotional abuse of power toward African Americans and Mexicans. Sheriff Ward humiliated the African American waiter at the bar in order to dehumanize him and gain control, and he gunned down the Mexican in order to maintain power. His police department, in their silence, quietly consented and permitted such injustices.

**Grading:**

The following grading criteria will be used:

1. Evidence that you clearly understand the intercultural concepts through your illustration and explanation of examples from the film.

2. The assignment is typed and neatly formatted.

3. A minimum of 50 words to illustrate and explain each concept.

4. College level language, grammar, and spelling. Papers with more than ten errors will be returned with no grade for a re-write. Re-written papers must be turned in within 10 calendar days thereafter, and a full grade will be deducted from its final grade.

# GROUP PRESENTATION: TOWN MEETING

**Purpose:** To engage in positive, constructive, and awareness-expanding education on multicultural relations through group interaction, role-play, formal presentation, and class discussion.

**Length:**    Part I:   10 minutes scene one, 10 minutes scene two

               Part II:  10-15 minute formal presentation
                              15-20 minute class discussion

               Total:   45-55 minutes

**Scenario:** You are a resident living in the town of Foothill. A series of hate crimes occurred in your town recently when swastikas and racial slurs were spray painted on the walls of a local church (attended mostly, but not entirely, by African Americans), homes belonging to Jewish and minority families who have been here for generations, as well as a "low income" apartment complex whose residents are American minorities, European Americans (whites), and recent immigrants from Asia, Central and South America, and Europe. A town meeting is called to decide on a course of action.

**Roles:** Choose from the list (not every role on the list has to be assigned, and there can be more than one victim of the hate crime). The mayor, law enforcement officer, victims of the hate crimes, teacher, parent, rich person, poor person, high school student, TV and newspaper editor, representative of the church. Let me know if your group wants to adopt other roles.

**Part One:**

**A. Scene One:** Role play (parody) the *least* constructive town meeting this group could possibly have. Base the content of your scene on at least 4 ideas discussed in *Chapter 3: Eight Ideas Concerning Cultural Relations and Racism in the United States Today.* In this scene the most ignorant, and the least sensitive and humane attitudes and behaviors towards people of other cultures come out. Base the town folks' communication on "aggressive communication" discussed in class. Let this scene be a realistic look at the many challenges facing cultural relations in the U.S. today. Do not use racial slurs or act out negative cultural stereotypes in your role play.

**B. Scene Two:** Role play a mutual learning, positive, constructive, and consciousness-expanding discussion by the town folks. Base the content of your scene on at least 4 of the ideas discussed in Chapter 3 (not necessarily the same 4 as scene one). Base the town folks' communication on "assertive communication" discussed in class. Consider using the ideas in Chapters 4, 5, and 6 as you decide with your group on a course(s) of action.

**Note:** In Scene Two, the town folks still have different opinions and experiences, but through effective communication skills, and overall solution-minded thinking, backed by action, progress is made. This is not to be a ". . . and everybody lived happily ever after" scene. The issues are still there, but the difference is in people's attitudes, communication, and actions.

**Part Two:**

**A. Formal Presentation:** Following the two scenes, your group is to deliver a 15-minute formal presentation, during which your group will a) identify the ideas your group chose to present; b) explain (teach) to the class the importance of considering these elements in intercultural communication and intercultural relationships in the U.S., or, in some cases, why you may have a different view than some of the ideas. Be thorough with your explanations. Use personal examples as appropriate to illustrate your points. Have everyone in your group take equal vocal part.

**B. Group Led Discussion:** Finally, members of your group will lead the class in a discussion related to your entire presentation. Ask the class a minimum of 4 questions. Sample questions: How can minorities feel safe in democracies where "the majority rules"? What societal forces might make some people racist and others open-minded and compassionate? Where would you turn for help in confronting an issue of intolerance? What are some reasons for people's indifference, and the impact of this indifference on society?

**Visual Aids:** Your group can utilize a variety of visual aids to enhance the quality of your presentation. This can include items such as props and costumes for your dramatic presentation, and charts for your formal presentation (if your group decides to use charts, please make sure they are simple to read, large enough to see from the back, and neat in appearance).

**Grading and Evaluation:** You will receive two grades for this assignment. A group grade will be given for the overall performance of your group, and an individual grade will be given based on your participation as a member of your group before and during your group's presentation.

**Group Grading Criteria:**

1. The thoughtfulness and insightfulness of your skit.
2. The organization and content of your formal presentations. Be sure to cover 4 ideas per scene, and include all role-played ideas in your formal presentation. Each member should cover part or all of one idea.
3. The preparedness and the degree of shared efforts (equal role-playing and presentation speaking time for every member).
4. Your group's ability to engage the audience in a discussion.
5. Length of your dramatic and formal presentations, and total length of your entire presentation.

**Individual Grading Criteria:**

1. Your regular attendance with your group during preparation sessions in class.
2. Your ability to use assertive communication skills in stating your thoughts and ideas with your small group members during preparation sessions.
3. Your ability to allow and encourage others in your group to contribute their ideas and thoughts (dominate or lack of vocal participation = poor grade).
4. Your preparedness for your dramatic and formal parts in the presentation.

**5.** That you share equal time (not longer, not shorter) with your group-mates in both the dramatic and the formal parts of the presentation.

**No Make-Up Group Presentations**

**Alternative Group Presentation (need to get permission first):**

As an alternative, you and members of your small group can develop a formal presentation (no skit) based solely on the *"Hollywood and the Media"* section in this book. If you choose this option as a group, you will present to the class a minimum of 10 examples of media bias and stereotypes towards people of different cultures and analyze them critically. Extensive reading and research will be assigned to you if your group chooses this topic. See me for details and grading criteria.

# DISCOVER YOUR FAMILY ROOTS / CULTURAL RESEARCH

**Length:** 5 to 7 minutes (no less than 5, no more than 7)

**Content:** You may choose one of the following three options for your presentation:

**Option #1:** Tell us the story of your cultural roots.

**Option #2:** Tell us the story of a particular cultural group in the United States. (Such as Persian immigrants/Persian Americans, African Americans, Irish immigrants/Irish Americans, Korean immigrants/ Korean Americans, Mexican immigrants/Mexican Americans, Russian immigrants/Russian Americans, American Indians, etc.)

**Option #3:** Describe the culture(s) of a particular foreign country. (If you pick this option, you must speak to me and get permission first. Generally speaking, you can choose this option if you have a compelling, personal reason for wanting to research a foreign country, such as if you're planning to study, live, or do business in a foreign country in the very near future.)

**Each option has two parts.** Be sure to allocate approximately equal time to both parts. Depending on which option you choose, organize your presentation as follows:

## OPTION #1

**Part I (Option #1 only):** Tell us the story of your cultural roots. Trace your cultural roots (one or both sides of your family) as far back as possible, to at least three generations before you. Include at least two of the following main points:

1. Where your family came from originally? Its history of migration. Why did it migrate? (Draw a time line or a family tree on a chart, if desired.)

142

2. Distinctions about your family culture as part of a larger culture: religions, customs, marriage, education, class level, trade (ways of making a living) unique family gatherings, special holidays or celebrations, rituals.

3. Social, political, economical, or environmental events which affected your family greatly.

4. Dreams, ambitions, hopes, joys, sorrows, or pain experienced by you, your immediate family, or generations before them as migrations, changes, or other circumstances became part of your lives.

To gather this information, you may want to be a detective of sorts and go on a history-finding investigation/excavation. Talk to family members, relatives, look though storage spaces for old artifacts, clothing, photographs, letters, etc.

Also, conduct some academic research into the subject matter. The three textbooks for this class will help. Do library research as needed and necessary. You can also ask me to suggest/ provide research material for your topic.

On your presentation day, tell the story of your own unique cultural roots to the class. Arouse the imagination of your audience by using your creativity to make your presentation as interesting and/or as thought-provoking as possible.

Part II (Option #1 only): Your personal experience/insight/ feelings in relation to your culture. After you're finished telling us your story, share with the class your own perceptions of your cultural heritage. Answer at least two of the following:

1. In what ways has your unique cultural heritage shaped and influenced who you are today? (Intellectually, emotionally, behaviorally, morally, socially, ethically, etc.) What do you consider unique and special about you because of your cultural background?

2. What are some things you appreciate and value about your culture? What are some things you don't agree with about your culture? Be careful not to generalize or stereotype your own culture; be specific and explain in detail why you feel this way, and point out exceptions and/or counter examples as appropriate, so the class can see the complete picture and understand why you feel a certain way.

3. Do you agree or disagree with Hofstede's cultural variables about your culture? If so, how? If not, why not? Be specific.

4. What are some unique challenges you face in the United States because of your cultural background? (i.e., fundamental human rights, stereotypes, glass ceiling, prejudice, discrimination, racism, internalized racism, ethnocentrism, etc.)

**Part I (Option 2 & 3 only):** tell us the story about this culture. Trace the history of this culture (If you are researching option 2, trace the history of this cultural group coming to and living in the United States). Include at least two of the following main points:

1. Where did this culture group come from originally, its history of origin and/or migration, and for option #2: why did it migrate to the United States? (Draw a time line or a migration route if desired.)

2. Distinctions about this cultural group: religions, customs, marriage, education, class level, trade (ways of making a living) unique family gatherings, special holidays or celebrations, rituals.

3. Social, political, economical, or environmental events which affected the culture greatly.

4. Dreams, ambitions, hopes, joys, sorrows, or pain this cultural group experienced as migrations, changes, or other circumstances became part of the culture's history.

To gather information, conduct fairly in-depth and detailed research into the subject matter. The three textbooks for this class will help. Conduct library research as well. You can also ask me to suggest/provide research material for your topic.

On your presentation day, tell the story of this cultural group to the class. Arouse the imagination of your audience by using your creativity to make your presentation as interesting and/or as thought-provoking as possible.

**Part II (Option 2 & 3 only):** After you're finished telling us the story of this culture group, share with the class your own perceptions of this culture. Answer at least two of the following:

1. What are some things you personally appreciate and value about this culture? What are some characteristics about this culture with which you disagree? Be careful not to generalize or stereotype; be specific, and explain in detail why you feel this way. Point out exceptions and/or counter examples as appropriate, so the class can see a complete picture and understand why you feel a certain way.

2. Do you agree or disagree with Hofstede's cultural variables about this cultural group? If so, how? If not, why not? Be specific.

3. What are some unique challenges people from this culture are facing in the United States (i.e., fundamental human rights, stereotypes, glass ceiling, prejudice, discrimination, racism, internalized racism, ethnocentrism, etc.)?

### FOR ALL OPTIONS:

**Presentation Delivery Style:** There is no reading from paper for this presentation, although you can write a simple outline on index cards and refer to them during your presentation. Most of your communication, though, should be speaking to the class.

**Utilize Visuals/Audios as Appropriate:** Show objects and artifacts (six objects maximum) from culture; bring/share food unique to your culture; utilize pictures, charts, drawings, clothing, maps, historical documents, music, and old photographs, etc. Pass them around if you wish. *Important:* if you pass objects around, be sure to label each item with a description so the class knows exactly what they see. Charts (written/drawn) must be large and clear enough for everyone to read from the back of the class.

**Grading:** Grading for your presentation will be based on:

1. The depth of research and information you present in part I (2 main points minimum)

2. The depth and quality of thought/reflection you present in part II (2 main points minimum)

3. Balance of time and effort between parts I & II

4. The length of your presentation

5. The overall communication quality of your presentation (Clarity of explanation, organization, audible voice level, neat and readable visual aids, no reading, etc.)

If you have any questions regarding this presentation, please see me.

## FINAL PRESENTATION:

### LETTER TO YOUR CLASSMATE(S)

**Length:** 3-5 minutes

**Assignment:** Write a letter (approx. 2 pages) to a classmate who is of a different continental cultural background than you. If your cultural background is bi- or multi-continental, please see me.

The purpose of the letter is to acknowledge *the difference this classmate has made for you, or to make a difference with this fellow classmate,* or both. Choose from among classmates or teaching assistants who have touched you, inspired you, helped you sort out difficult issues, and/or helped you learn and understand more about yourself and others. You can also choose to write to more than one classmate (at least one of whom is of a continentally different cultural background), or to the entire class.

**On your presentation day:** Read your letter to your classmate(s) in front of the class. Acknowledge publicly how this person has touched you and made a difference for you.

The following sentence completions can help you think about what to write to this person:

- My experience with you in this class has been . . .
- What I learned from you (about myself, about people who are different, etc.) are . . .
- I have come to realize that . . .
- I felt (inspired, touched, understood, loved, validated, supported, etc.) by you when . . .
- I felt (saddened, hurt, pain, unjust, etc.) when I listened to your experience about . . .
- Something I would like to tell you about my experience is . . .
- What's difficult for me to acknowledge is . . .
- I'm trying to understand why . . .
- What I want to say to you, but have been afraid to is . . .
- As a member of my cultural background, I will . . .
- As your friend and ally, I will . . .
- I want my friends and allies to . . .
- My hope for my children and yours is , and what I will do as a parent to help make this happen is . . .
- A classmate whom I've been nervous to talk to this quarter is . . .
- What I want to say to my small group is . . .
- My experience in this class has been/what I want to say to my fellow classmates is . . .
- What I would like to tell the president, faculty, and staff at Foothill College is . . .

**Acknowledgment Cards:** Bring cards & envelopes to class to write feedback to your classmates on *all* presentation days. You can buy them at a stationery store, or make them yourself. Please bring cards that show thought and care on your part.

**Grading:** Grading of this presentation will be based on

1. The length of your presentation
2. Preparation
3. Overall thoughtfulness and effort of your presentation. Also, as a member of the audience, if you write acknowledgment cards for the speakers on all presentation days, credit will be added to your class participation grade.
No make-up presentations

*". . . And so it is that the moment you pledge your highest love, you greet your greatest fear."*

*—Neale Donald Walsh*

"Everything now, we must assume, is in our hands; we have no right to assume otherwise. If we do not falter in our duty now, we may be able, handful that we are, to end the racial nightmare, and achieve our country, and change the history of the world."

—James Baldwin

# Selected Bibliography — Books

*The Diary of Anne Frank,*
by Anne Frank

*A Different Mirror: A History of Multicultural America,*
by Ronald Takaki

*Gandhi,*
by Louis Fisher

*A History of Multicultural America: Minorities Today,*
by William Loren Katz

*Latinos: A Biography of a People,*
by Earl Shorris

*Long Walk to Freedom,*
by Nelson Mandela

*My First White Friend,*
by Patricia Raybon

*Race, Class, and Gender: An Anthology,*
by Margaret Anderson

*Strangers from a Different Shore:*
*A History of Asian Americans,*
by Ronald Takaki

☛

# Selected Bibliography — Films

SPECIAL INTEREST FILMS:

*A Class Divided* (PBS Video, Frontline )
The famous "brown eye, blue eye" experiment, and
a class reunion.

*The Color of Fear* (Stir-Fry Productions. Oakland, CA)
Eight men of European, Latin, African, and Asian decent
discuss racism.

*Not In Our Town* (California Working Group. Oakland, CA)
How a small town in Montana successfully fought
against hate.

*Skin Deep* (Iris Films. Berkeley, CA)
College students from across the country meet to
discuss race issues.

*Stolen Ground* (Stir-Fry Productions. Oakland, CA)
Men of various Asian decent discuss their experience
with racism.

FEATURE LENGTH FILMS:

*Gandhi*

*Get on the Bus*

*Lone Star*

*Malcolm X*

*To Kill a Mocking Bird*

*Notes*

*Notes*

*Notes*

*Notes*